Heddi

Calr

With very many thanks to Stepfamily, the National Stepfamily Association, and to the family whose photographs appear in this book; without their help and generous involvement this book would not have been possible.

Stepfamily
The National Stepfamily Association
Chapel House
18 Hatton Place
London EC1N 8RU

Information: 0171 209 2460
Counselling Service: 0990 168 388

First published in 1996 by
A & C Black (Publishers) Limited
35 Bedford Row, London WC1R 4JH

ISBN 0 7136 4542 3

A CIP catalogue record for this book
is available from the British Library.

Printed and bound in Great Britain
by Hunter and Foulis Ltd, Edinburgh.

My Two Families

Althea

Photographs by Richard Clemence

A & C Black · London

Do you know anyone who is part of a stepfamily?
Lots of children live in stepfamilies, but all stepfamilies
are different. The people in this stepfamily would like
to tell you what it is like for them.

This is a photo of Drew, Charlie and Lizzie, with their father, Kevin. Most of the time, the children live with their mum and their stepfather. But every other weekend, they come to stay with their father, their stepmother Annie and her two daughters.

Louisa and Judy are sisters. Louisa is the older and Judy the younger. They live with their mum, Annie, and their stepfather, Kevin. On some weekends, they go to see their father.

When all the children are together with Annie and Kevin, they make one big stepfamily. They have been part of a stepfamily for three years now. It took a while for them to stop feeling shy with each other and to become friends.

Lizzie and Drew say it was quite strange when their parents split up.

Lizzie says, 'When Mum and Dad first told us they were splitting up, it was like a dream. It didn't feel real. Mum took us to live with our stepfather John.'

Drew says, 'I think it was worse for Charlie because he was younger and he didn't really understand what was going on. He wanted his Daddy.'

After Judy and Louisa's mother and father separated, their father moved out. Judy says that after her dad moved out, she, her mum and her sister lived on their own.

'Louisa was away in term time. So then it was just Mummy and me. She liked me to help with the shopping and cooking, and she played games with me.'

'Mummy made lots of new friends, and we spent time with them at weekends. Sometimes we all went out for the day, and that was fun. But sometimes they just sat drinking coffee and talking for hours on end. That was boring!'

Things changed when Annie met Kevin. Judy and Louisa got to know him. Judy says, 'When he came to live with us, we did things together. Sometimes Lizzie, Drew and Charlie came for lunch. We started going on outings all together.'

If you have had one parent to yourself for a while, you may not want to share them with someone else. Louisa didn't like it much when Kevin first came to live with them, but she trusts him now. She finds he is a great help when she has a problem to sort out.

It can take a long time to get to know new members of a family and make friends with them. It might be a while before you feel you can really trust them.

Drew says, 'When we first started spending weekends all together, we watched television with Louisa and Judy, but we didn't play with them. We played our own games and they played theirs.'

Judy says, 'This is my Daddy. I go to stay with him every other weekend. Louisa comes too in the holidays. He spoils me and lets me eat pizzas and gives me presents. My Daddy has some girlfriends. I like some of them, but sometimes I feel a bit shy of them.'

Judy has got used to having both a father and a stepfather, and she likes it now. She says, 'You never know, my Daddy might get married again one day, then I would have a step-mummy as well. I love both my daddies.'

Louisa enjoys going to stay with her father, but she's not so sure that she wants to have a stepmother. 'I suppose it depends on whether I like his girlfriend or not - some of them are fun.
It might mean we would have to share him with other children too. That would take some getting used to!'

All the children have had to get used to having new stepbrothers and sisters. Judy says, 'When Drew, Lizzie and Charlie first came to stay, we all stayed well apart. Then we had a water fight and found we were all playing together. We still felt quite shy of each other though.'

Judy adds, 'It was great when I found they really did want to play with me. Now Drew says "hello" to me when he comes to stay, and he really seems pleased to see me.'

Now that she has got to know Charlie, Judy loves having a stepbrother of her own age. 'It's not like other friends,' she says, 'I have had to get to know the inside of him before I could really be myself with him. Sometimes we squabble, but all families squabble at times.'

When two families get together, it instantly makes a bigger family. It might be necessary to make some new rules. In this stepfamily, no one is allowed to be in anyone else's bedroom without asking. Judy and Charlie are in the bedroom that Charlie shares with Drew, but Drew has said he doesn't mind them playing in there.

Charlie shares a bedroom with his brother Drew, in this house, and in his mum's house as well.

Charlie likes having someone to play with in both his homes. He says, 'We have a baby at my other home. His name is Tom. I was excited when Mum got pregnant. Lizzie and Drew do things together at home, so I'm glad I have Tom to play with there. Here, I have Judy.'

It can be difficult if you have to share a bedroom with a stepbrother or stepsister who is very different from you.

Lizzie says that she had to share a bedroom with Louisa for a while. 'She woke up very early and went to bed late. I couldn't get enough sleep! It's good that I've got a room of my own now. I need my own space where I can be quiet, to do my homework and things. I know I'm lucky, other stepchildren have to share. My friend Sophie has to share a bedroom with her two stepsisters. She has got a cupboard in her room though, where she keeps all her own things.'

Louisa said, 'I tried to stay quiet after Lizzie told me. But the next morning, I didn't realise the clocks had changed, so I still got up really early, and started doing my piano practice!
I think Lizzie has forgiven me now.'

Sometimes it's useful to get together as a stepfamily and talk about everyone's different needs - though it's not always easy. Annie says that they often have meetings, to discuss anything that is important to them as a family. It gives everyone a chance to say what they feel about things. 'At one meeting, I asked my stepchildren what they wanted to call me, and they said that they liked calling me Annie.'

Sometimes children call their step-parents by their names at home, but call them Mum and Dad when talking about them at school. It's easier than having to explain all the time.

Children in stepfamilies have to get used to different routines in each home. Lizzie says she didn't find this a problem. 'We soon learnt what to do when we came here.' Lizzie and Drew say that they keep their two lives separate. They don't tell each family what they do in their other home. 'It stops there being any upset.'

Louisa says, 'There aren't too many rules here, except, "No shoes on the new carpet!" I have to vacuum it if I forget. Mummy shouts at the boys if they fight too much.'

Annie and Kevin find that sometimes when all five children are together at home, everyone gets a bit short-tempered. They think it's a good idea to go out and do things together, and so they arrange lots of outings. Drew is very keen on sport, so when he's playing football, they all go to watch him.

This time they are playing netball on the beach. It gives them all a chance to run about and let off steam!

Kevin and Annie think it's important for the children to have some time with their own parent. Kevin looks forward to the weekends when his children come to stay.

On those Friday evenings, Louisa and Judy are away, and Annie goes to visit a friend. This means that when Lizzie, Drew and Charlie arrive, they can have their father on his own for a while.

It gives them the chance to tell him about their fortnight and talk about anything that's more private. They go on some holidays together too.

Annie takes Louisa and Judy away on outings as well. It gives her time to talk just with them. Louisa likes having time alone with her mum. She makes her mum and Judy laugh, and they have fun together.

It gives Louisa and Judy the opportunity to talk to their mother when she has time to really listen to them.

Judy likes the fact that she can talk to both her parents, and her stepfather. 'I am lucky to be able to talk to both Mummy and Daddy about the things that upset or worry me. Sometimes it's difficult to know how I feel, but I can talk to both Daddy Gordon and Daddy Kevin.'

Last year, Annie and Kevin got married. Louisa played the organ at the service. Lizzie played a clarinet solo.

Drew and Charlie read some prayers.

Judy was the bridesmaid and carried the flowers.

All the children say there are advantages to being part of a stepfamily.

Louisa says she had always wanted to have more brothers and sisters, so she likes being part of a stepfamily.
It means that there is always someone to talk to.
She enjoys doing things with Judy and Charlie - like watching their favourite television programme together.

She adds, 'I can play with the little ones, or I can talk about more adult things with Lizzie sometimes - she's almost exactly my age.'

All of the children enjoy Easter, because they get twice as many Easter eggs as they used to.

They all have two Christmases as well. They spend one day with one parent, and one day with the other. They have a lot of new relatives, and they get quite a lot of presents altogether!

Being part of a stepfamily is not always straightforward. But after everyone has had some time to settle down and get used to their new relationships, it can work very well. As Judy now says, 'Being in a stepfamily is one of the best things that ever happened to me.'